14 PROMPTS

WRITING PROMPTS FOR SURPRISING
CREATIVITY

JOE BUNTING

ISBN-13: 978-0-9884497-6-3

ISBN-10: 0-9884497-6-5

Published by The Write Practice

thewritepractice.com

❀ Created with Vellum

ALSO BY JOE BUNTING

Hands: A Short Story

————

How to Write Short Stories Series

Let's Write a Short Story: How to Write and Publish Your First Short Story

15 Days to Write and Submit a Short Story: a Writing Workbook

How to Win a Writing Contest: From Idea to First Prize

————

Free Books

10 Steps to Becoming a Writer

30 Tools to Write, Publish and Market Your Books

Book Launch Map

Beauty is mysterious as well as terrible. God and the devil are fighting there and the battlefield is the heart of man."

—*The Brothers Karamazov* by Fyodor Dostoevsky

WHY WRITING PROMPTS?

Just after college, I dated a poet from Washington whose most remarkable quality was her voice. It went up and down like a child's, and she enunciated her T's and K's. When she said even simple things like "thanks" or "hi," her voice made me feel like everything around her dripped with turquoise glitter.

One night, we took a walk downtown, strolling too far away from the coffee shop where we had gone to talk. The farther we walked, the more my voice began to match hers. Wonder, I discovered, is infectious. Soon we found ourselves miles from where we had started and on a seedy side of town. I had never walked there before, and everything looked new and strange. She was the pied piper, I the child lured by her voice.

Our relationship didn't last long. She went home to Washington. I left to travel the world. I will never forget how I spoke around her, though; how easily my voice fell into pitch with hers, and how the change caused the whole world to transform, as if my voice cast a spell that made everything I saw glow.

I only realized later that the source of her power wasn't her voice but her eyes. The voice can only speak what the eyes see, and the greatest tools you possess as a writer are your eyes. I'm not talking about the two painted spheres on your face, but your lenses, your perspective, your worldview. If your eyes see the world dripping with wonder as spider webs drip with dew, your writing will show it. If your eyes see corruption and deceit behind every closed door, you will write like a conspiracy novel. If your eyes see a young boy walk onto your train, a scar on his forehead and a wand in his hand, you will be J.K. Rowling. We write what we see.

This is not your average book of writing prompts. In fact, it can barely be called a book of prompts. When packaged into books, prompts come in batches of between 1,000 and 5,000, and are often just lists of ideas or first sentences or even just one or two random words. If you are looking for a regular book of prompts, I recommend *1,000 Creative Writing Prompts Box Set* by Bryan Cohen, which can be purchased wherever ebooks are sold.

But this book does not have 5,000 prompts. Nor does it have 1,000. It has only fourteen prompts. Why so few? Because this book is more an exercise in seeing than a list of ideas to get your story started. Like the Washingtonian who taught me to see the world through turquoise-glittered lenses, I hope this will help you see the world, and thus your writing, from a new perspective.

There are inevitably writers who have done this

better. I think immediately of Annie Dillard's *The Writing Life*, which you should immediately purchase before you read another sentence. But we don't write because we are the best at something. We write because we write and sometimes we don't know why.

Lastly, I hope you are encouraged to pass on this gift of seeing. You are not just a writer, you are an artist; one who paints portraits of the world as no one has ever seen and then asks others to stand behind your shoulder and gaze upon them and be changed. You pass your lenses to others. I hope you will pass lenses full of joy, hope, and love; lenses that can see life through the deepest darkness. This is our great calling.

How To Use this Book

Over 100,000 people have read this book. For some, the writing this book inspired was the first creative writing they had ever accomplished. For others, it was a welcome return after a long season without writing.

My hope is that anyone who picks this book would be compelled to write, no matter your education, lack of creativity, language, or skill level. All of us can become great writers through practice. May this book become part of *your* practice.

The chapters and exercises found in this workbook were originally published and expanded from thewritepractice.com, a website dedicated to helping writers develop their artistic eye, finish their books, and get published. Every weekday, you can find a new writing lesson paired with a writing prompt, and each day, we invite writers to respond to the prompt for fifteen minutes, posting their writing on the website. The following fourteen "chapters" follow the same pattern.

The lessons on thewritepractice.com are excellent, but the best part of The Write Practice is the writing from readers like you. There, our community has shared incredible writing—writing that will someday soon be part of bestselling novels, impactful poetry, and memoir that will make you laugh and cry and learn new things about the world.

I have also seen plenty of writing that is just plain terrible. Which is, of course, why we take part in these kinds of exercises: to learn to sort our pearls from our pig fodder. Part of developing the sight of a writer is learning to spot our own mistakes, and often, others are the first to point out both our greatness and weakness before we can begin to see for ourselves.

That's why the following exercises are meant to be done within a group. The Write Practice functions as a perfect community for feedback, and if you like, after you finish each exercise, you can go online and share your work on the corresponding lesson. However, if you would like to go through this workbook with your writing group, or if you want to team up with a few writing friends, it will work just as well.

On thewritepractice.com, writers spend fifteen minutes on each prompt, but for the purposes of this book, I suggest writing for thirty minutes. As a timer, a phone, watch, or cuckoo clock will work just fine.

I also recommend choosing to write with pen and paper as you follow at least some of these prompts rather than typing on your computer.Typing and handwriting use different parts of your brain, and you might find you can be more creative while writing by hand.

Good luck with the writing prompts that follow, and always, happy writing.

1

OUT OF PLACE

I don't know if it was the black eyes of the people watching me or the way everything looked dark and overused in that city, but I was ill at ease, as if restlessness could be defined by a leg that wouldn't stop bouncing under the table and an imagination that predicted I would be mugged.

I sat in a fifties-style diner and waited. I waited for half an hour, forty-five minutes, an hour. I felt like I had been waiting for people all day.

But then he showed up, his dark hair in small dreads, loose-bound behind his head. He was black but had sounded Hispanic over the phone. He sat down in front of me.

"Sorry for being late," he said. "Your wife told me about what happened. You want to see it?"

He showed me the merchandise, that nefarious thing I'd driven to the city for, the thing I couldn't live without.

"It looks good. I'll take it." I pulled out my checkbook.

"Whoa...no no no, we only do cash here. I thought I was clear about that on the site."

"I didn't see the site."

"Right, yeah, I'm sorry about that, but we only do cash."

"I don't have cash," I said, my stomach sinking, as it had been all day.

"I don't know then. You could come back tomorrow, or..."

"I'm not coming back tomorrow. I can get cash. Can you meet again in 45 minutes?"

"The banks are closed, man."

"It's fine."

I hit up the grocery store first, dropping a half-dozen bagels on the dirty conveyor belt in that dim-lit place. "What's your cash back limit?" I asked.

"One hundred dollars," said the checker.

"Great," I said. I didn't care that she did not smile, that her face bore the creases of tiredness, or the fact that she did not say, "Have a nice evening," as I left. I cared only for my need.

The bank was next. I pulled my daily limit. With that, and with what I already I had, I thought I would have enough. And then it would be home and out of this dark city where no one knew my name. I called him.

He sounded surprised to hear from me, as though he thought I would flake out of the deal. He asked me where I was. I told him. He said he wasn't far, that he would meet me in the parking lot of a coffee shop on 7th Street.

When I pulled in, he was already there, his tall figure in my headlights cutting a column of light against the black night. I parked illegally and he sauntered over, pulling what I wanted out of the bag and handing it to me. I put the merchandise in the front seat and handed him the dirty cash. He counted it in the parking lot, then shook my hand and left.

Driving home, I put my hand on it, feeling its soft metal purr, that touch that you only get from something you've longed for too many hours in darkness.

When You Feel Out of Place—Write

The story above is about my trek to Atlanta to buy a used computer I found on Craigslist. The whole time, I felt like I was in *The French Connection* doing a drug deal. Thus, the *film noir* feel of the passage and the ambiguous "merchandise." I felt out of place. I spent eight hours in a city I didn't know very well, waiting for people I didn't know at all.

I read somewhere that the best time to write is when you first arrive at a new place, whether that's a new country, city, or even restaurant. Everything is fresh and new and strange. You don't have those lenses over your eyes that tell you what to ignore and what to notice. We writers can be social misfits. While sometimes that's uncomfortable, it gives us a creative edge. When you're an outsider, you see things others don't.

When have you felt out of place? How can you capture that experience in words?

————

THE PROMPT

Write about a time you felt out of place, awkward, and uncomfortable.

Try not to focus on your feelings, but project your feelings onto the things around you (for example, in the story above, I talked about darkness again and again because I felt confused and uncomfortable most of the day).

Set your timer for thirty minutes and write away.

Good luck!

DISCIPLINE

When writing, it's common to experience huge emotional highs followed quickly by bottomless emotional lows.

"Wow. This writing is amazing," you think as you read back. "If I don't win a Pulitzer for this, I'll be shocked."

And then, a few days or few hours or a few minutes later you read something you've written and cringe. You get knots of frustration in your shoulders and a tight squeezing in you stomach because what you've written is so bad you feel physical pain just to look at it.

Writing can make you feel crazy.

And the emotional turmoil can easily distracts you from continuing to write. You can get so sucked up into how you're feeling that writing becomes a distant priority.

Write anyway. Write when you feel like you're a terrible writer. Write when you feel like you're the best writer in the world. Don't stop to feel bad about yourself, and definitely don't stop to bask in your ego. Discipline is doing what you *should* do even when you don't feel like it. Feelings will change, but your writing will last forever. Don't trade what is permanent for something that will change tomorrow. Write.

5 Mental Tricks to Stay Disciplined

The only secret to writing is to write. Don't go back and fix your spelling mistakes. You can do that later. Don't google that quote from the famous author you absolutely need. You can do that later. And for goodness sakes, don't "take a break" to check email and Facebook while you wait for inspiration. You won't find inspiration on Facebook.

This is the daily trudge of the writer. You have to write when you love what you're writing and just want to soak up every word. You have to write when you hate what you're writing so much it's throwing your back out. This daily trudge is so difficult that every once in a while I invent a new aid to stay focused.

Here are a few mental tricks to help you escape the emotional cycle of writing:

1. Close your eyes.

When you're feeling down about yourself and your writing, the worst thing you can do is read the last sentence you wrote.

Instead, close your eyes and type. You can fix it later.

(Here's a tip offered by one reader: if you are using a standalone monitor, turn the screen off while you write.

If not, just tape a dark piece of paper over the screen. Just make sure you don't move your hand an inch to the left.)

2. Give yourself a time limit.

Set a timer for fifteen to thirty minutes and write as much as you can during that time. Don't edit. Don't re-read. Don't play Facebook games. You can do that stuff after the alarm rings out. This is a great way to force your brain to focus for solid chunks of time.

3. Write with a typewriter or by hand.

Typewriters and notebooks don't have the internet. They don't have FreeCell or Spider Solitaire. All you can do is write or not write. On top of that, these mediums force you to separate editing time from writing time, which can slow you down.

4. Take breaks.

Many people think the longer they sit at their computer working, the more productive they will be. The truth is our minds and bodies need breaks from time to time.

Go on a walk. Stare out the window and zone out for five minutes. Do some pushups. Meditate. I try to do this for twenty minutes, twice a day. Breaks help our subconscious catch up so that we can refocus on our work.

5. Invent your own way to focus.

This short list isn't meant to be complete. You can easily invent your own tricks to focus. The principles are always the same. Focus on writing. Review later. Avoid distraction.

When you do this, you can get ahead of the emotions that distract you. Stop being a bi-polar writer. Start being a productive one.

How do you deal with the emotional cycle in writing? And what do you do to stay focused?

———

THE PROMPT

Practice focus by writing about a basketball player before a big game. How does he prep his mind? Does he visualize the game in his mind? Does he think about what it felt like the first time he played the sport?

Choose one of the tools above to help you focus (personally, I'm going to write with my eyes closed).

Write for thirty minutes.

YOUR VOICE

I asked a bestselling novelist how long it took him to find his voice.

Four or five novels, he said.

If the average novel is about 100,000 words, then you have to write 400,000 to 500,000 words before you find your voice. That's about 1,000 blog posts, 450 newspaper columns, or 80 short stories.

And how many have you written?

The first step to finding your voice is to write.

Agents and editors who read thousands of manuscripts a year say they can tell when an author hasn't discovered his or her voice in the first pages of a manuscript, sometimes in the first paragraph. Those who haven't go into the slush pile.

Your second step to find your voice is to listen to feedback.

You share your writing with a few people. This is where a critique group, writing workshop, or online community like The Write Practice Pro is helpful. They read your writing. Then they tell you what they liked and what they didn't. You learn what you can. You discard what isn't helpful. Over time, the feedback makes you a better writer.

When you're first starting, you need a lot of feedback. That's because you haven't found your voice yet. Later, after writing 500,000 words or so, you won't need as much feedback.

Until then, you write. You share your writing. You ask for feedback and you learn to take it graciously.

There are no shortcuts to this. There is only practice.

So get writing.

Have you found your voice? If not, how many books have you written? blog posts? short stories? If not, how fast can you write four or five books so you can find it?

———

THE PROMPT

Let's twist things up. You show up to Mrs. White's Tudor style mansion to meet with your writing critique group, as you do every week. You expect to have a fun time talking about writing and getting feedback, not to find one member of the group murdered in the drawing room.

First, describe how you find the murder victim. Then,

after the police lock you in a room with the rest of the guests, write about your suspicions of who-dunit as you look around the room at your fellow writers.

Do I need to tell you to set your timer for thirty minutes anymore?

THE 5 TYPES OF SENTENCES IN A STORY

I t's easy to be a writer. All you need is five types of sentences. These five sentences make up every story ever written.

Let me show you. And since we're talking about story in this chapter, why don't we begin with one? As you read, see if you can identify the different types of story-telling sentences.

It was a cold night in September, and a group of us were huddled around a campfire telling ghost stories. First, Jenny told a creepy story about a serial killer. But then it was Tommy's turn.

"A few years ago, in this very campsite, a young boy and his father were sitting in a fire just like this, when all of a sudden..."

"Tommy, no!" I said.

"What?!"

I couldn't stand it. I already knew what

was coming. This was the exact same story Tommy had told on our last camping trip, and it was just as lame then.

I put my head in my hands as Tommy continued.

"The boy and his dad heard some sticks snapping at the edge of the fire. And then..."

I felt like I was going to throw up in my mouth. This wasn't happening. This couldn't be happening again.

I stood up, walked over to Tommy, and punched him in the arm as hard as I could.

"What the?!" he said. "Why did you do that?"

"You know why," I said. "You should be ashamed of yourself.

My hand stung, but I felt good for standing up to the evils of bad storytelling.

Every story ever written is built with five types of sentences:

1. **Action.** What are your characters doing?
2. **Dialogue.** What are your characters saying?
3. **Description.** What are your characters hearing, touching, tasting, and smelling?
4. **Inner monologue.** What are your characters thinking? How do they feel?
5. **Exposition.** What information does the narrator want the reader to know?

Here is the story above tagged with its element:

> It was a cold night in September, and a group of us were huddled around a campfire, the smoke clinging to our clothes as it climbed to the stars. DESCRIPTION
>
> We were telling ghost stories. First, Jenny told a creepy story about a serial killer. Then, Blake told a funny story about toothless vampire. But then it was Tommy's turn. EXPOSITION
>
> "A few years ago, in this very campsite, a young boy and his father were sitting in a fire just like this, when all of a sudden..." DIALOGUE
>
> "Tommy, no!" I said.
>
> "What?!"
>
> I couldn't stand it. I already knew what was coming. This was the exact same story Tommy had told on our last camping trip, and it was just as lame then. INNER MONOLOGUE
>
> I put my head in my hands as Tommy continued. ACTION
>
> "The boy and his dad heard some sticks snapping at the edge of the fire. And then..." DIALOGUE
>
> I felt like I was going to throw up in my mouth. This wasn't happening. This couldn't be happening again. INNER MONOLOGUE

I stood up, walked over to Tommy, and punched him in the arm as hard as I could. ACTION

"What the?!" he said. "Why did you do that?" DIALOGUE

"You know why," I said. "You should be ashamed of yourself. DIALOGUE

My hand stung, but I felt good for standing up to the evils of bad storytelling. INNER MONOLOGUE

Five types of sentences, but how many are you using?

Writing that makes use of only two or three of these types of sentences makes for unbalanced, stagnant prose.

Each type is necessary, each serves it's function. In the example above, description sets the scene. Exposition gives the reader important information. Dialogue draws us into the story. Inner monologue helps the reader relate. Action provides the conflict.

Together, you have a balanced story, but if you leave any out, a story can get problematic fast.

Different writers will focus on one or two of these types of sentences more than the others. Stephenie Meyer focuses on inner monologue. Ernest Hemingway focuses action. Cormac McCarthy focuses on description. Shakespeare, as a playwright, focuses on dialogue.

Part of discovering your voice is finding your particular balance within these five sentences. Still, all those writers understood and used each of them. Even Stephenie Meyer has some action, dialogue, and description.

Another important thing: most literary writers tend to avoid exposition. Use too much and you'll be accused of "telling" rather than "showing." Exposition is the mayonnaise of storytelling. It can make for a moist, delicious sandwich, but too much will trigger your gag reflex.

Which sentence type do you gravitate toward in your writing?

―――――

THE PROMPT

Write a campfire story. Try to use all five types of sentences. Write for thirty minutes.

WRITER'S BLOCK

I spent most of this morning trying to figure out what to write. I had four or five different ideas, all of which I threw out.

I was blocked.

As I thought about it, I realized there were three reasons I was blocked:

1. Someone I respect criticized my writing.
2. Shortly after, I didn't get a writing job I wanted.
3. Then, a writing mentor of mine said a piece I had written as a favor "needed a lot of work."

Taken individually, none of these would have been that big of a deal, but together, they sent me down a shame spiral.

"It's true," I thought. "I'm a terrible writer. I have no taste. Everyone can read my writing and see how much I suck. *Yada yada yada. Shame shame shame.*"

The hardest part of getting over writer's block is to realize you're blocked. Once you know you're sick, it's pretty easy to prescribe the medicine you need to get well.

What is the medicine?

The cure to writer's block is to write the worst sentence in the world.

In Hollywood, a psychologist named Barry Michels charges screenwriters $375 an hour to fix their writer's block. He once told a writer to kneel in front of his computer for one minute every day, praying to the heavens to help him write the worst sentence in the world. The screenwriter thought it was stupid, but he did it. A few months later he had written an Academy Award-winning screenplay.

Why would you want to write the worst sentence in the world? And how could that cure your writer's block?

Write the worst sentence in the world because it frees you from perfectionism.

Writer's block is caused by your irrational desire to write the *best* sentence in the world.

I wasted two hours of my morning because I was trying to write the perfect sentence—or rather, a lot of perfect sentences—sentences that wouldn't be open for criticism.

Perfect sentences aren't just impossible to write, pursuing them will destroy you. Instead, write something real, open, and vulnerable.

Write the worst sentence in the world because you can't inspire yourself.

There is no such thing as genius. In fact, inspiration itself doesn't come from you.

The bestselling author Elizabeth Gilbert said in her TED Talk:

> The Romans didn't actually think that a genius was a particularly creative individual,"They believed that a genius was this magical divine entity who was believed to literally live in the walls of an artist's studio, kind of like Dobby the house elf, and would come out and invisibly assist the artist with the outcome of their work.

Inspiration, in other words, is a gift from something outside of you, and if you write terribly, the best part is, it's not your fault. If you realize at a deep level that the responsibility for the quality of your writing rests with something outside of you and beyond your control, it will free you from the performance anxiety that causes writer's block. Freed from the outcome, all you can do is show up, sit at your computer, and write the worst (or best) sentence in the world.

Write the worst sentence in the world because it's impossible.

Writing the worst sentence in the world is just as impossible as writing the best sentence, but for some reason, when you intentionally aim to do something awful, terrible, simply no good, it frees you to do your best work.

If you give yourself permission to be a sucky writer, you allow yourself to be great.

How do you get unblocked? What techniques do you use to cure writer's block?

————

THE PROMPT

Our goal today is to write the worst sentence in the world.

I hope you have spelling and grammatical errors. I hope it is boring. I want you to write something so bad that when people read it they think, "This guy or girl is the worst writer I've ever read."

In order to write the worst sentence in the world, write for thirty perfect-free minutes. Then, go through your writing and look for the absolute worst sentence you wrote.

When you've found your worst sentence, have the courage to share it with your writing group or on thewritepractice.com. If nothing else, it will give everyone a good laugh, and it will likely cure your writer's block.

6

YOU MUST REMEMBER EVERY SCAR

"The only requirement," to be a writer, said Stephen King, "is the ability to remember every scar."

I have a few scars (and you do, too). There's that girl in the eighth grade, my father's illness in the seventh, and that boy earlier than that who told me to shut up every time I spoke to him.

When did I learn to fear my voice?

The true writer enters into wounds. Sometimes she enters into her own, often into the wounds of others, and occasionally even into the wounds of people she makes up.

The writer enters into wounds because she knows when she confronts the wound, she will discover the secret of life.

(Wounds turn into beautiful scars).

What wound do you need to confront?

————

THE PROMPT

Tell the story of one of your scars. You don't have to share this with your writing group, but I'm sure they would be honored if you did.

(You know how long to write for.)

7

BRUSH STROKES

W hen my college Literature professor told us Hemingway would write all day in small Parisian cafes, and afterward take his lunch to the Musée du Luxembourg where he would look at paintings by Cézanne, it transformed how I looked at writing forever.

In college, I read Faulkner, Dostoyevsky, Tolstoy and all the other writers infamous among college students everywhere. The authors, I imagined, were like statues in a museum—old, cracked marble, missing limbs, dust piled atop their heads. They were empty-eyed faces carved into cathedral stone, looking down on us to make sure we knew their names. If we misremembered, they would denounce us before God at the golden gates.

But my professor's story humanized them. I pictured Hemingway sipping cups of French coffee at a cafe with black and white pictures on the wall, writing slowly, with lots of cross outs. I saw him with his sack lunch, made by Hadley, drinking out of a thermos (did they have those in the 1920s?), and tracing Cézanne's brushstrokes with his eyes. He had intense blue eyes.

Writers, I realized, were not part of an evil plan hatched by professors to torture their students, but real people, with real ambitions and insecurities.

I realized then that writers were trying to give something to me, some greater perspective of the world maybe. Or even just an enjoyable afternoon.

The purpose of this book is to transform. I don't want to give you techniques. I want to transform the whole way you approach writing.

When I began learning about Hemingway's life and influences, it helped me to realize that if I wanted to transform the way I approached writing, I needed to see myself as part of the tradition. There is a great continuum in this art form, an inheritance that all writers can and should apprentice themselves to.

But there is something unique about Hemingway. He didn't apprentice himself just to writers. He looked to a painter to transform his work.

"I'm trying to do the country like Cézanne," he said, "and having a hell of a time and sometimes getting it a little bit."

Hemingway tried to learn how to write from a painter. What did he learn, you might ask.

I'm not an art historian, but I do know Cézanne believed in using big bold brush strokes. Some of his paintings could have been done with a You can see this ethos in Hemingway's writing. Some have called Hemingway's prose childish and simplistic, but his genius was his use of a few strong words to do so much work. His prose is full of action, not décor, as if he was painting bold words with a big brush.

Our eyes are the most important tools we have. Our eyes tell us what's important to write and what to leave out. You should study other writers, surely, but don't forget other art forms. They too can help you shape the lenses with which you view the world.

What if you studied an artist, molding your lenses around hers, and then practiced seeing like she sees, writing like she would write? How would this change your writing?

————

THE PROMPT

Find a painting by an artist you admire, and study it for several minutes. What is unique about his style? What emotions does the painting evoke? Who are the characters (paint, light, and architecture count as characters), and how are they portrayed? Are the scenes incredibly detailed, like Dickens or Hugo, or are they spare and modern, like Hemingway? Are they surreal, like Vonnegut? How does the painter see the world? You may want to verbalize the answers to some of these questions in writing.

Next, try to imitate the painting with your writing by

describing the scene around you as that artist would. If you want, maybe even go outside with your laptop or pen and paper. Like Hemingway, you might have a hell of a time with it, but it also might give your writing a unique edge like no one else's.

8

BE STILL

Sometimes when I am walking well, it feels like I am still. Instead of moving through the world, the world moves around me. The cold fall morning slides by—the sky sprinkles on my face, the back of my neck, the bare skin on my hands. Leaves that displayed themselves proud on their branches on Sunday are now, on Monday, piled up on the sidewalk. The grey sky is framed now by bare branches and the soldier who stands guard over the town square is no longer veiled by leaves.

I walk still and the world moves around me.

A young man rides a lime green bike toward the coffee shop. He wears a black balloon vest so baggy he could fit four of his skinny frame into it. His black hat is turned sideways.

The first time I saw him, a few months ago, he swaggered into the coffee shop, a cigarette between his lips. I wondered how long it would take for Vicky to kick him out. There was no smoke coming from the cigarette, though. Just a little mist. He took a puff and the tip lit up LED red.

As he leans his bike against a newspaper box I wonder. What is his life like? What are his dreams and where did he learn to swagger? Where did he buy that balloon vest—did he fawn over it when he first saw it?

And of course, would he make a good character in a novel?

These are the thoughts you can afford when you're still. If you walk too quickly you scare them. They fly away like frightened doves.

Be still today. A writer cannot afford to scare away inspiration.

When was the last time you were still as a writer? How did it feel? How can you be still today?

––––––

THE PROMPT

Take a deep breath. Then breathe it out. Take another. Exhale it. Where are your shoulders? Are they tensed over the keyboard? Loosen them. Is your neck tight? Let it relax, bowing over your fingerpads which are feeling the texture of your keyboard or the scrap of paper you write on.

In a moment, I want you to close your eyes and begin to write. But first, breathe in clean air, tasting it as it passes over your tongue. Exhale the long strands of cobwebs that tie up your spine and clutter your brain. Big breaths now. Watch those spider webs disappear into the air. Nothing exists but your spine and your breath and your fingers hovering over keyboard, holding all potential in their tips.

When you're ready, close your eyes and begin to write.

9

BIRDS

The window in my living room opens out to a wide field that ends in a stand of trees. The birds live in the trees, and in the mornings, they fly out over the field.

There's something about birds.

Sometimes you see a yellow one or a blue one. Mostly, though, they are shades of white and brown. I watch as two white birds chase each other, loop around, and fly out of my view.

Some people spend hours watching birds. I imagine it sharpens their senses. Their eyes learn to pick out flashes of movement in the overwhelming green of the canopy. Their ears learn the distinct song of each bird.

I, however, am content to watch the field from my living room window, and if a bird flies through my view, so be it.

Bunting is what you do in baseball (as I have heard all my life). It is also that red, white, and blue striped fabric they put up in half circle shapes to be patriotic. Best of all, to my mind, though, Bunting is the name of family of birds.

Why is it that birds feel like hope and joy and a kind of unity with nature that I've experienced only a few times? Why is it that they feel like my soul?

Just now, a yellow bird flew by my window, the whole length of it, and the crossed the field in long dives and disappeared into the yellow trees beyond.

———

THE PROMPT

Birds can add a touch of detail that lights up your writing. Today, practice writing about birds. If it would help, go outside with a notebook and a pen and look for them. They're everywhere.

As you describe the birds you see, think about what they mean to you.

10

BUSY

"An aesthetic experience is one in which your senses are operating at their peak, when you're present in the current moment, when you're <u>fully alive</u>," Sir Ken Robinson said.

When was the last time you felt like that? When was the last time your writing made someone else feel like that?

Most of us, though, are not having an aesthetic experience. We are having a *busy* experience.

A reader sent me an email recently, "I want my writing to be a way of *crystallizing* reality,"

I love that. What if you're writing could crystalize reality, distill a day into a paragraph, a lifetime into a book?

Today, for me, is a busy day. I have to wash my white shirt. I need to make an emergency run to the cleaners. My wife is stressed. I'm stressed. I'll be running around like a busy fool today.

A trip to the dry cleaner is not the stuff of literature,

and it's impossible to create anything interesting in a rushed state of mind.

However, these busy days often have the most potential for stories to spawn from them, if you're paying attention. Having a lot to do isn't the same thing as being busy. Busy is a state of mind.

How do you write when you have too much to do? Here are a few tricks:

1. Carry writing tools with you (or steal them).

On the day of my wedding, I found a napkin, stole a pen, and while my groomsmen were carrying in the keg, I sat on a couch to write out my thoughts and a few key images (like the half-dozen bees circling those beautiful purple flowers right next to the chairs where our guests would sit, or the thin crescent of the moon just peaking above the pines and poplars).

Everyone says their wedding day was a blur, that they don't remember any of it. I, on the other hand, wrote everything down, and I'll never forget those small details.

Leave the house without a pen and paper to your peril!

2. Find moments to escape.

No matter how rushed the day is, there are always a few minutes here or there. (Confession: In emergencies I've excused myself for a long trip to the "bathroom" to get some notes on paper.)

Don't apologize or feel guilty for being sneaky. It will be worth it later.

3. Write while waiting.

Most busy days have moments of "hurry up and wait."

I once ran through Budapest to catch a train only to find out it didn't leave for six hours. So what did I do? I sat down on the gum-stained cement ground inside Budapest's beautifully run-down train station and wrote.

There are always moments to write. You just have to be disciplined enough to take advantage of them when they appear.

4. Practice the art of haiku.

Haiku is a form of poetry invented in Japan consisting of one five-syllable line, one seven-syllable line, and one five-syllable line. It's short, and thus perfect for the rushed writer (you can even publish your haikus on Twitter).

"Real haiku," a reader told me, "is not just an exercise in counting syllables. It forces you to channel your thoughts and experiences down to their essences. It's hard to do this if you can't become present in the moment."

Here is a haiku from a reader that I enjoyed:

> *a shadow drifts*
> *across polished wood grain, then*
> *fades into silence*

So much in just twelve words! You're never too busy you can't write twelve works.

5. Wake up.

To be an artist of any kind you must make a commitment to consistently "wake up" to the moment.

You have a busy day ahead of you. Tomorrow will be busy. The next day will be busy. There is no alternative but to wake up, to write right now, to recreate your crazy busy life and the crazy busy lives of others into art.

Of course, this is why we do art in the first place, to be more present, more awake, more fully alive.

Have you been present today? What do you do to "wake up"?

———

THE PROMPT

Reflect on your busy day and on the present moment. Write about it.

11

THE SOLDIER AND THE MAN WHO WAS SICK

Today, I heard the story of a man named Ed who has Lou Gehrig's disease. Doctors told him he had two to five years to live. Ten years later, he is still alive. It's something of a miracle. However, sometimes he can't button his shirt on his own, his hands are frozen stiff and turned inward in strange shapes, and he talks slowly, like a man whose voice has almost run out.

When his son was sent to Iraq, he said, "Enough is enough, God."

What was to be done, though?

He and his wife drove his soldier son to the airport.

"I think he was trying to be brave," Ed said.

In the back seat, there was the soldier, the stoic.

In the front, watching him and fearing for him, sat the father, the disabled man whose vulnerabilities were visible before all the world.

We all have these two people inside of us. You are strong, but you are also weak. You are stoic and brave, but you are also vulnerable and afraid.

We are all disabled men and women whose vulnerabilities are there for all the world to see (even if only *we* see them).

And we are all trying to be brave.

It's 10:57 PM. I'm sitting on a friend's couch in Chicago. Next to me a pile of books is splayed across the red couch pillows. Today I rode Colleen's racing bike through the city, past brick building after brick building. Some of them looked like castles and were obscured by beautiful trees. Some were bare and dirty. I loved them all. I am here for a writers conference. I like coming to these once in a while because it reminds me that I have a story that matters. You have a story that matters, too.

In fact, our stories can change the world.

However, right now I'm having a hard time believing that. It's late. I'm tired. I'd rather not be writing now. The words I'm writing are not very good. I don't have anything to teach. My voice feels like it has long run out. But at least I'm here, being brave. This is the battle going on inside of all of us, writers or not. It's a battle between the stoic soldier and the vulnerable, disabled one. A good writer, I think, gives voice to both.

Who do you prefer to write about? The strong or the vulnerable? The powerful or the weak? Why?

———

THE PROMPT

Write a story about a disabled man and a soldier. What do they say to each other? How do they interact?

12

YOUR CITY

"I guess when you're a poet laureate you're a poet for a particular group of people," Paul Willis, the former poet laureate of Santa Barbara told me. "It makes you think of the whole community, and how poetry can be part of their lives."

What if you wrote for your city? To your city? How would that change your voice?

Poets once were the servants of kings and princes. They wrote the histories of the people, speeches for the great events, and sometimes, when the occasion called for it, a good ol' fashioned drinking song.

In a way, their words were food for the community.

I once wrote a prose poem to a group of friends. Sitting around a table full of Italian food, I read it to them. Never has anyone listened so intently to anything I've written. Since they knew it was for them, for them alone, they engaged with it more deeply than if it were written to some abstract audience.

"Life isn't a support system for art," said Stephen King. "It's the other way around."

What if you made yourself the unofficial poet laureate for your city? What would you write?

———

The Prompt

Write something for your city. What will you say? How will you support the life of your community?

13

FALL

I looked at the tree, so yellow it looked like a column of sacrificial fire. It was just one tree in a line of them at the edge of a brown field. The other trees were green and brown. This tree was among them but not of them. I looked at the tree unblinking until my eyes watered and shut tight of their own volition. I was afraid.

The night sky fell and turned my skin blue-grey and my skin goosebumped with cold then smoothed over like an ice cube but still I stayed outside, crouching, then kneeling, then lying prone like a sniper staring at the yellow tree which was disappearing into the night.

The grass around me was dry, and when the wind blew, it whispered to me but I could not understand its language. The crickets and frogs and even the soft songs of birds spoke but in words I did not know.

"What are you saying?" I said to the birds.

"What are you trying to tell me?" I said to the dry grass.

"And you, column of fire, what do you mean? I can't

understand you but if I did I think I would do it different.
I would be different."

But they were silent, and when the light was finally
gone I got up and went home.

The next day the leaves on the tree were gone, fallen
to the earth.

What are your surroundings saying to you?

———

THE PROMPT

Two choices:

Think of an autumn memory. Choose one detail from
that memory and describe it. Continue writing for 30
minutes.

Go outside. Describe the most arresting thing you see.
Then continue writing for 30 minutes.

THE MYTH

P erfect is no place for a writer.

　　Listen to me: you will never write a perfect novel, short story, essay, blog post, sentence. Everything you write will be criticized. If it's not, then it has been ignored.

Your job is not to write perfect sentences. Stop thinking it is.

No one will praise you. They will either ignore or criticize you. (Even if you are lauded, you will care more about the criticism than the praise.) That is your fate if you want to write.

I want to write. So I will write pieces that are open to criticism (even from myself). Pieces I know are imperfect. I will publish them anyway.

You have to write something you're not an expert in. You have to begin the novel you aren't ready to begin. You have to write the blog post that is immature and incomplete.

This idea that you will be perfect is a myth. It is a lie

from the enemy of creativity, the one who wants to destroy your life.

You will never be perfect.

This is a good thing, of course, because your readers aren't perfect either, and how could you ever relate to them in your writing if you were perfect? People don't need you to be perfect for them. They need you to be so completely honest about yourself and the world that they realize they are not alone. There's someone out there who gets it.

(There will be those who demand perfection and are disappointed when you don't measure up. Slough them off like a too-large jacket. You don't need them.)

The opposite of perfectionism is vulnerability, and vulnerability is the source of joy.

So it comes down to this: do you want to be perfect or do you want to be happy?

———

THE PROMPT

The most vulnerable (and therefore interesting) people are children. Describe a child, either one you know or one you've made up.

Write for 30 minutes.

THIS MOMENT

Since I started The Write Practice, I've talked to thousands of aspiring writers, writers who would kill for the chance to live off their sentences. Making a career out of writing is a noble dream, and I don't blame them for dreaming of it, but what is nobler still is the person awake to the breeze on a cool fall day; the person who can hear joy in a child's voice; the person who can look out at the morning filled with that haze and half-light that mornings have; who can see the silhouettes of trees, the outlines of birds; who can hear the birds and the crickets and the life of morning, and see them. Just see them. Really see them.

How can I convey what it is to see? How can I show you that there is nothing more than this moment and that it is good?

While the stories we write may end, our writing isn't over until we quit or die. That is because writing's main function was never just to entertain, instruct, or communicate. It was never just for making money. Like breathing, writing is meant to serve your life. There are also moments when writing turns to toil, as does everything set at by human hands. I've been a professional writer for many years now, and there are moments when it's easy to forget what a gift it is to be able to write every day.

But in those perfect moments, when all the conditions are right, writing enables us to see.

Thank you for reading. Thank you for writing. May you never stop.

BECOME A WRITER

Maybe you write because it makes you feel alive. Maybe you once read a book that made you think, "It must feel amazing to write something like this. Maybe *I* could be a writer." Maybe you feel like you can't *not* write.

So then, how do you do it? How do you become a writer?

Get the Free eBook: My free book, *10 Steps to Becoming a Writer* contains the the best pieces of advice I've learned on how to become a writer.

Get the book for free here: thewritepractice.com/writer

ABOUT THE AUTHOR

Joe Bunting is an author and the founder of The Write Practice, where he leads a community of creative writers and teaches courses on how to write books and get them published. He lives in Atlanta.

www.ingramcontent.com/pod-product-compliance
Lightning Source LLC
Chambersburg PA
CBHW032121280326
41933CB00009B/941